VIA Folios 136

Dear Pat i
Eileen
The copyright
Sorry, is missing.
page But I thank you
for being a pal?
our community at
Yorville. With love and
gratitude –
R. Twktsor
Watson

Italian Kisses

CONTENTS

This book is for Connor Noah Watson and Clara Emily Watson,
my wonderful grandchildren.

Our sister Debbie, our Mother, and Grandma Water

INTRODUCTION

When my grandparents came to America, they brought with them the values and customs from "the old country." We were raised to believe in family. From grandma were learned her secret recipes by using "a little of this and a pinch of that." We also learned the value of kind words, and why Italians kissed on both cheeks—one kiss to keep, one to give away. Grandpa taught us clamming, planting, and the sacredness of his fig tree—which grew from a twig that crossed the ocean with him.

Many years later I came to understand grandma's rose-colored words. Uncle Abertino was never called a philanderer, but rather a man with a tendency. Uncle Ben was not an alcoholic, but rather a man with a condition. And for Zia Agatha there was just one word—*pazienza*—accompanied by the sign of the cross, a shrug of the shoulders, and hands outstretched to the heavens. Grandma's words had more power than the *Baltimore Catechism*, which we memorized before making our First Holy Communion.

And Grandma was always proudly there to pick out our white dresses or dresses for special religious occasions. She said we had to look pure and holy just as all the saints. For many of us growing up as "war babies" stories about the lives of the saints were more popular than fairy tales.

It is my wish that my own children—as well as the children and grandchildren of my sisters, Lois and Debbie, will find this book offers a way to reminisce about holidays. Although our family often recreates Italian family moments—and in terms of love we succeed—memories of "the olden days" frequently elude us.

Hopefully this book will help our children and grandchildren come to understand how family and our Italian heritage blesses our lives.

I. WINTER WONDERS INTO SPRING

Circa 1930: My mother, Clara (Ciara), Grandmother, Nancy,
Aunt Chris, Uncle Frank, Grandpa, and Aunt Rose

Sunday dinner with Grandma and Grandpa

Every Sunday was a feast of food and, for Grandma, all the cooking that she did on Friday and Saturday was her passion and her mission. On Sunday, when people gathered around the table, she would study our faces looking for signs of contentment.

Then just as we were about to take the last bite of her homemade pasta, she was there heaping a second helping onto your plate. With a smile, she would say: "You see, I knew you were still hungry. Grandma always knows. Just save some room for dessert."

Meals were always sumptuous. But unlike Easter Sunday, there was no leg of lamb, nor a variety of pies. Instead, we often had roasts, tender veal cutlets, meatballs, and a dish of *braciola*, thinly cut rolled steaks. *Braciole* had centers of garlic, parsley, pine nuts, prosciutto, and Parmesan cheese. These were tied with string and cooked for hours in the tomato sauce that would become a thick blanket to cover the homemade ravioli or lasagna.

As I think of those days, I can see why Grandma and Grandpa had so many Saturday afternoon opera tiffs. When Grandma wasn't standing in the kitchen cooking, she would sit by the radio and crochet. But Saturdays were a tug-of-war between cooking and the opera. Grandpa was hard of hearing and would not wear a hearing aid. As such, their arguments often had a familiar ring. When he came to the operatic arias that he loved, he would turn the volume up and begin singing loudly and off key.

Grandma would emerge from the kitchen, wiping her hands on her apron and say, "Anthony, we have a house on the water for peace and quiet. Now you are scaring the seagulls away."

In the next breath, she would add: "Anthony, turn that down. How can I think and cook at the same time?"

If he still ignored her, she would go into the parlor with her arms waving in the air as she cried out: "*Silenzio!*"

He would counter with "Annunziata, *aspetto un minuto*," meaning that he expected her to wait until the aria ended. He called her Annunziata only when he was very serious about something.

Or he might wave her off with "Nancy, *aspetta*" at which point she would walk away shaking her head saying, "He never listens." However, when he called her "Nancy" he was listening—just not immediately.

Gram would say, "I'll be glad when the warm weather comes. He'll be out in the garden and I will have some peace and quiet in here."

It was during a holiday at my sister Lois's house, that the photograph book of memories reminded us of "the olden days" at Grandma and Grandpa's for Sunday dinner at noon. Relatives and friends always joined us. One photo of our grandparents with our mother, her two sisters and brother perfectly portray their Sunday best for church and then home again for a seriously food-filled day.

The too tall Christmas tree challenge

The upside-down wedding cake chandelier adorned the entrance parlor in Gram and Grandpa's house on the water. Each year during the first week of December, Grandma would send us to the attic to bring down boxes of Christmas ornaments. She liked to inspect each one and then decide how many new snowflakes to crochet for the tree. Even though we always had a small tree under the chandelier, she liked to make extra snowflakes to replace those that she thought "looked tired."

Then she would sigh, "When Papa sees us with these boxes he is going to say, 'Annunziata, that tree in the middle of the parlor is in everyone's way.'"

By the second week of December, Grandma sent Grandpa and his brothers to cut down a tree so it could "settle" into the parlor. One snowy afternoon we waited for the tree to arrive, but Grandpa pulled the car into the side garage. Then we heard him on the stairs stamping snow from his boots. When Gram opened the door, he said, "Nancy, before we bring in the tree, I have something to say. The tree farm would not allow anyone to cut down small trees this year. So, I brought you the smallest of the big trees and a surprise very, very small one."

Gram suspiciously went to the windows to catch a glimpse of what Grandpa's brothers were bringing into the house. "Mamma Mia," she cried out. "That tree belongs to 'Jack and Beanstalk.' How will it fit under the chandelier?"

As his brothers set to work fitting the tree onto the stand, they moved directly to the semi-circle of window seats. Gram cried out, "No, not there."

But Grandpa surprised and stopped her. "Look. I bought you a beautiful baby white tree with bubbling candle lights to put on your table in the center of the parlor."

Before she could say a word, a white tree with attached tiny candle-stick lights replaced the vase of flowers. Then Grandpa went under the table to the central floor plug, and with a flip of the switch, bubbling colors danced from the tree to the chandelier crystals.

Grandma was so overwhelmed that she said nothing. She smiled and became a bit teary-eyed. Then there came another surprise. Onto the live tree that touched the ceiling along the window by the long bench, the men strung white snowball bulbs made by the Sylvania Company. Once plugged in, the snowballs changed into an array of pastel shades.

"These are the future," Grandpa said.

"Nancy, you always tell the children that we find a solution to every problem. This is our Christmas tree solution—one tree for you and one for me." Then he went over to her, pinched her cheeks into a smile, and gave her big kisses.

Grandma grinned saying, "Now, enough kisses, Anthony. I'll have to get busy crocheting more stars. Our first floor-to-ceiling tree will need three times as many snowflakes." Then, to us she said, "You see, just when you think your husband never listens, one day you find that he hears you after all. You just need to be patient."

Our Mother's Tree with Grandma's Crochet Snowflakes

Christmas 1944

Christmas with my secret mission Army dad

During World War II, my father missed my first Christmas. When he was able to come home the next year it was apparent from photos that the celebration was lavish. A tall Christmas tree standing on a window bench was the living room highlight that our mother remembered decorating.

"Grandma was so happy for us that she made certain her daughters placed one strand of tinsel at a time on each branch, so the tree would be perfect," she said.

At the opposite end of the window bench there was a manger, crafted in Italy, which Grandma kept up until Epiphany on January 6, a feast commemorating the arrival of the Three Wise Men.

As the first grandchild, I was born when my mother and her two sisters lived at the Water House. Overlooking Long Island Sound, it had a wrap-around porch where they could sit, listen to buoys clanging, and talk about their men who were either overseas or stationed in Florida during the war.

The Sunshine State had become a military training ground. When enemy U-boats sank at least 24 ships off the Florida coast near Miami and Jacksonville, a special group was formed to prevent further attacks. As a pilot, our father often talked of flight operations dispatched from Florida bases. But there was news blackout. And today there are conflicting stories from museums as to why the military did not want people to know that there was a war going on here in the states.

But once my father came home, even for a short leave, it was a celebration. Grandma once said to me, "When your father arrived home, it really felt like Christmas. There were so many toys in our living room that it looked like a department store. You wanted to play with everything at once. The stuffed giraffe was your favorite, even though we all thought you would want to hug the teddy bear, just like your father kept hugging you."

She added, "But you were so excited to show him that you knew how to walk that you just wiggled out of his arms and raced along the living room, staying close to the window seat for support."

However, I later learned that in my enthusiasm, I lost balance, reached for a branch and the tree with all its decorations tumbled down. Grandma was so concerned that I could have been hurt, to protect me—and future *bambinos*—she decided there would no longer be tall trees, just a small one on a sturdy table. And it remained that way until I was about 10 years old.

Struffoli Day: An Italian family tradition

On the Sunday between Christmas and New Year's Day we had a tradition that came to be called Struffoli Day. It was the Italian family Christmas for all of our relatives. No one asked what foods they should bring; they simply cooked a favorite dish.

But one year, in addition to a main dish, everyone brought a bowl of struffoli for dessert. Made from bits of marble-sized dough, struffoli are deep fried, then drenched in honey and covered with colored sprinkles. Quite unexpectedly, this day of family love turned into a bit of rivalry.

Grandma explained, "My mother made a large bowl of these on Christmas Eve for sweetness after our traditional meal of the Seven Fishes that always included *puttanesca*. It was basically spaghetti with anchovies, capers, fresh Italian parsley, garlic and olive oil."

Grandpa said his mother built the *struffoli* up on a platter into the shape of a Christmas tree, just as he had taught Grandma. Grandpa chimed in, "Then starting at the top, using our fingers, we popped them into our mouths one at a time."

Each year Gram's *struffoli* tree seemed to get taller. The year of the unintended bake off was the year she considered her dessert to be a work of art. With so many people bringing *struffoli*, she placed the bowls on a sideboard with little dishes for individual servings, as these were picked up and eaten like little pieces of candy. Then just before dinner Gram made a grand entrance with her *struffoli* tree sprinkled with multi-colored nonpareils and laced with silver tinsel. The family applauded.

Grandpa's sister, Zia Agatha said: "Annunziata, your *struffoli—che belle dolce*. We should keep it as the centerpiece and eat the others. You know that with a Christmas tree shape those morsels will be dry as a bone by dessert time. I know this because our mother's *struffoli* were always dry."

Then turning to Grandpa, her brother, she said, "Isn't that right, Anthony?" He shrugged.

Gram turned away and simply said to all the women, "Let's bring out the meal." Almost like magic, an endless stream of food trays and dishes filled two dining room tables.

Once everyone sat to eat Grandpa said the grace. Then expecting Gram's words to be: "Now let us enjoy our family and this feast," she instead said, "I've placed cellophane over the *struffoli* tree to keep it moist. And next to my tree there is a crystal bowl of honey and shot glasses filled with toothpicks. If you think my *struffoli* are too dry, you can stick them with a toothpick and dip them into the honey. Now we thank you again, Lord. Amen."

And at that moment we were certain that not a single person in that room—except for Zia Agatha—would dare to put a toothpick into Gram's crunchy Neapolitan delight.

Grandma's Recipe from our mother's book, "Nanny's Table"

STRUFFOLI INGREDIENTS

3 cups flour plus a pinch to make up for the liquor

2 teaspoons baking powder

¼ cup sugar

3 eggs

1 teaspoon lemon zest or chopped lemon candied lemon peel)

1 large lemon, zested (about 1 and 1/2 teaspoons)

3 - 4 tablespoons of orange juice

1 tablespoon limoncello

1 tablspooon vegetable oil

COOKING PROCESS

Combine ingredients and roll into a long log shape

Cut into 1-inch pieces and roll into balls

Drop balls into hot frying pan that contains 2 ½ inches cooking oil

Fry until light brown

Remove and drain on paper

When all the balls are cooked, toss them in a generous amount of warm honey

Arrange in a pretty glass dish and add colorful sprinkles

Circa 1940: Clara Rose Mercugliano

Grandma's rose-colored words

From her mother, Grandma learned the art of euphemisms and kind words. "Bless instead of curse, because curses come home," was a favorite saying of hers. Grandma may not have seen the world through rose-colored glasses, but she spoke as if she did, even though her body language sometimes betrayed her. Our philandering great uncle was never called a "casanova." Instead, Grandma talked about his "tendency" while shrugging her shoulders, lifting her hands upward and raising her eyes to heaven.

My late 97-year-old Aunt Rose recently explained: "Uncle was tall and handsome with thick, black, wavy hair. The twinkle in his blue eyes was his downfall. The girls were all in love with him. And he had the tendency to please. He didn't want to hurt their feelings. Once he married, Aunt Georgia straightened him out, but every now and then his tendency returned."

As family lore goes, one day, Uncle entered the family pastry shop hugging a young, giggling bank teller. It seems that Aunt Georgia was helping in the back kitchen at the pastry shop that day. When she heard his voice, she gasped, "the tendency." Zia Agatha, the pastry shop matron, dashed from the kitchen waving her rolling pin. The young lady fled and, after that experience, Uncle began taking trips to Italy with his brothers. He claimed his doctors said that exercising in the old country was good for his heart.

Another uncle had what Grandma dubbed "the condition"— Grandma never used the word alcoholism. She said he developed "a condition" after his wife died. "It broke his heart," Grandma would say, "and blackberry brandy is a healer."

Apparently, tendencies and conditions were not unique to our family. A colleague from a large Italian family remembers an older cousin, "Tony, the painter," who missed family gatherings for three years. Whenever anyone asked, "Where's Tony?" the matriarch answered, "He's painting a house." No one dared mention that it was "the big house, up the river."

Another euphemism we often heard was quietly spoken when a wedding was called off either by choice or because a father deemed that young man was not suitable for his daughter. We never heard, "He stood her up" or "he left her at the altar." The words used were "*È scomparso*," meaning, "He disappeared." Today we call that "ghosting."

Although some relatives whispered, "She's better off without him," or "She deserves better," no unkind words were spoken in our house. Grandma's advice: "The Good Lord always wants us to think of people as good. See people like they were the roses in your mother's cheeks."

San Giuseppe Day at the pastry shop

Because Saint Joseph's Day is Father's Day in Italy, when growing up I spent the night before the feast at our grandparents' house to celebrate. The next day, March 19, I helped at the pastry shop. For that entire day everyone made just *zeppole di San Giuseppe*, special cream filled fritters. Even if it was a school day, I was excused by the nuns as a favor to Grandma and Saint Joseph.

This was the only time that Grandma left her kitchen to work at the pastry shop alongside her sister-in-law. Shaking her head, she sighed, "I can put up with her all day only this one day a year to help Papa on Father's Day." In reality, she looked forward to the *zeppole* bake-off with Zia and her cousin Lucille. Each had a special recipe for making the custard-like ricotta cream that filled the deep-fried fritters.

The original *zeppole* recipe, recorded in the 1830s by a Neapolitan duke, was similar to Gram's fried dough rounds which she topped with tomato sauce or, as a treat, sprinkled with powdered sugar.

At Grandpa's shop the men whipped up fresh batches continually. Grandma liked her *zeppole* to resemble cream puffs. Zia and Lucille preferred the more traditional wider circle which they filled with a mountain of custard cream topped with a Maraschino cherry.

Gram put extra filling in her puffs and on the top, there were swirls of cream reaching for a dark Amarena cherry. Her secret ingredient was Limoncello, a liquor that her brother brought her from the old country. Zia used lemon zest with bits of candied fruit whereas Lucille favored orange zest.

Gram was so protective of her Limoncello that she poured it into dark brown cough syrup bottles which I guarded in my schoolbag. Once at the shop, I sat at an ice cream table in the front doing my homework. Then when she would peek her head through the kitchen door and motioned to me, I would bring Gram her prized liquor. When she did this, if she noticed that the lines with customers seemed to be too long, she would prepare a tray of cookies. Then my job was to pass the tray to those waiting for their *zeppole*.

Although Gram willingly made the cookie trays, nonetheless, she whispered, "The way people waited for St. Joseph to work a miracle to break the famine in Italy, these people can wait to eat a perfectly fresh pasty that honors him."

By the end of the day all three women called themselves the bake-off winner based on watching people's facial expressions as they tasted their miniature samples, which adorned the tops of the glass pastry shelves.

"Not a one left," Gram smiled at Grandpa at the end of the day. "But I saved these for the good sisters." Then while packing two dozen *zeppole* to bring to the convent of the Sisters of Mercy, she reminded me, "When someone does you a favor, as the nuns do for me, Papa, and St. Joseph, always remember to show them your appreciation by bringing them a gift."

Zeppole de San Giuseppe or Grandma's fried dough recipe

Grandma reigned as the "Pizzagaina Queen"

Grandma's kitchen was a sacred place where she baked, cooked, and tightly held her culinary secrets. Essentially, she was "a little of this and a pinch of that" type of cook. While she often let us roll out the dough for her homemade pasta, only as Easter approached did she bring us into her flour-filled world. It was also the only season of the year in which Gram encouraged relatives to share a piece of their "pizzagaina," the Neapolitan pizza rustica.

Although Gram was convinced that no one could compete with the texture, moisture, and meats in her treasured recipe, she was always on the look-out to be certain that she remained unrivaled. On the Saturday before Easter her in-laws and cousins came by for the women's brunch and exchange of their hearty pies. As they arrived, she would whisper to us, "No matter what the others taste like, be sure you say something nice."

When the church bells rang out at noon on Saturday, Gram placed her prize on the dining room sideboard and waited for the family. As each one arrived with their dish, she placed them on either side of her own masterpiece. For Gram, the best part of the brunch came after the last relative had said, "good-bye." Her twinkling blue eyes would light up. It was time for her pizzagaina critique. We can still picture her taste testing.

"Zia Agatha always uses too much mozzarella. I could tell this was hers with my eyes closed. Lucille's is still too watery. This one is from Aunt Georgia. I don't even have to taste. Just look how she skimps on the meat.

"And Antoinette, can you imagine she used boiled ham instead of baked ham? And look at this one. Millie claims she made it herself, but this is her husband's. When he comes to the pastry shop to help out, he always makes the crust for the cream pies too thick."

As she went down the line tasting each version, Gram became ever more convinced that she still reigned as "Pizzagaina Queen." Once satisfied, she would percolate a pot of demitasse. Then we would sit at the window seat watching for Grandpa to come from work to reclaim his home.

"We have a lot to be grateful for," Gram smiled. "It's a lot of work, all this cooking. But this is what keeps family together."

Italian Ham Easter Pie, Pizzagaina, from Benjamin Jude
Ardito, a grandson who carries on the family tradition

PIZZAGAINA INGREDIENTS

1 ½ lbs. prosciutto or prosciutini

1 ½ lbs. baked ham

1 stick of pepperoni

Cut the meats in small cubes and set aside in a large bowl

In a separate bowl combine:

1 ½ lbs. Ricotta cheese

1 ½ basket cheese (probably only found in Italian neighborhood shops)

12 eggs

1/8 cup of olive oil

Add ham cubes to the mix, sprinkle with coarse black pepper, set aside

The crust:

4 cups flour

1 cup shortening

2 tsp. baking power

2 eggs

A pinch of salt and pepper

COOKING PROCESS

Roll the dough to a thin layer and line the bottom of a pan or baking dish

Pour mixture into the dough

With the remaining dough, make long 1 inch strips and place them on
     top in a crisscross design

Bake at 375 degrees until golden brown

My mother, Clara Rose, in 1942.
She was 22 years old in this photo.

Memories of lilacs, brides, and bocce

Late-blooming lilacs, biscotti, bridal bags and bocce balls were signs of June at Grandma and Grandpa's house. Although Grandpa's garden was filled with vegetables, he made certain that there were flowers blooming. Grandma believed that houses close to the water should have flowers to counter the salty air that settled into walls and carpets. "Too much salty air makes the house musty. Even with all of my baking, those sweet aromas can't fill the rooms upstairs."

Grandma liked the double white peonies because of their lily of the valley scent. For color, she arranged them with dark pink peonies. To the side, there was often a small vase of roses. However, Grandma said our mother's room was like a lilac garden.

"When your father was home on leave [during World War II], they went walking one day. He broke off a lilac sprig and put it in her hair. She held onto that lilac for days before pressing it into a memory book."

In June, there was often a friend of our mother and her sisters getting married. Grandma would proudly say, "They always wanted me to make the tray of biscotti. They said mine were better than any pastry shop, even Papa's. Of course, mine were better. I used flavorings from the old country, which are too expensive to make to sell in a store."

Our mother and her sisters decorated the large trays with Jordan almonds, Italian candies and strands of tinsel. At receptions, it was traditional for brides and grooms to pass a tray of cookies to their guests. The bride usually wore a satin drawstring bag on her arm. After guests took the biscotti, they would open the bag and add a card with a cash gift. Because our mother's friends knew that Grandma could sew beautifully, they often brought her fabric to match their gowns so that she could make their bridal bags unique by adding lace, seed pearls, or even a crochet fringe.

Grandpa also loved late May and June. After having spent May planting his gardens, which forever needed tending, he took time for his favorite sport—bocce ball. Grandpa made a court on natural soil on the side of the house and planted tiger lilies within view, so Grandma could enjoy looking at flowers while the men played their games.

Grandpa had said to her, "Nancy, I don't see you all day. At night, when I am home playing bocce, I like for you to be there to watch."

As Grandma explained, "What was I going to say? He takes good care of this family. So, I sit and watch and enjoy the flowers. He looks over, smiles at me, and sometimes throws a kiss."

II. SPECIAL SPRING AND SUMMERS

Creating a time for Grandma kept her mind off the war

Today we have get-togethers and parties, but when Grandma would reminisce about a large gathering of food and family, she called the event "a time." My younger sister, Lois, gathered old family photos into a pictorial family history. Looking through it again the other day, there were photos of our Mother's beach parties with her coworkers from the telephone company.

Grandma often talked about those gatherings. She said the girls would create "a time" to take her mind off her worries about the boys at war. "And what did I do all day? I cooked for them," she both pouted and smiled.

Technically "a time" was more than just a gathering, it was a term associated with a significant event. When our Mother talked about creating "a time" at the Water House, she said they would find an excuse to make it special. Party excuses ranged from letters from fiancés, to someone announcing talk of marriage, or a celebration for one of the women receiving a promotion.

Perhaps the best description of "a time" is portrayed in the book by Dr. Ed Iannuccilli, *Whatever Happened to Sunday Dinner*. His father defined "a time" as parties after graduation, a wedding ceremony, funeral, or Holy Communion. But during the war, Mother and her sisters stretched the meaning to include an old-fashioned good time even on late summer days.

The Water House was a perfect place to gather because its front lawn stretched to the beach. And there was never a need for a rain date. Between the wrap-around porch and the entry foyer with its window seats, 30 to 40 people could comfortably party and enjoy Grandma's cooking.

Grandma told us, "I would make my fried pizzelles, pour fresh-cooked tomato sauce over them and then add shredded mozzarella. You should see how those girls gobbled them up. And my stuffed artichokes—they couldn't get their fill."

Apparently, these were just snacks. No gathering would be complete without Grandma's fried sausage and peppers, her homemade ravioli, and eggplant Parmesan. I can just hear her say, *"Mangia. Mangia.* This will put some meat on your bones."

Then, as she did with us always, after heaping seconds of ravioli onto our plates, she would remind us: "Save some room. Papa will be home soon with the Italian pastry."

But to her partying daughters, their girlfriends, and a few men who did not make the Army, our aunt said Grandma would add: "Until Papa gets here, *mangia.* It will take your mind off your worries. And trust the good God to bring our boys home. Then just wait and see what a time we will have."

*Circa 1943: Mother with her friends
from the Telephone Company.*

*July 1946: Top row is great-aunti, Grandma, and Nanny,
my father's mother. My mother, center, top step.
Centered on the first step, there I was, the birthday girl.*

My third birthday celebrated at the Water House

Memories of celebrations at Grandma and Grandpa's big house on the water still bring a smile to my face. They lived in a house on Beach Street, which had a large wraparound porch and a widow's walk at the top. As I was going through our photo albums on a snowy weekend, I came across a photo of my third birthday. At the top of the stairs, there stood three Italian matriarchs with Grandma in the center. My mother, with her long black hair, was seated in front of her. And I was centered on the first step surrounded by seven mothers and eight children smiling.

When I think of our life there, I can almost see the stories unfold. I still remember walking up the stairs, touching the columns, and getting to the double doors to the parlor. However, when growing up, we never had to open the doors ourselves—Grandma was always there to greet us.

When our parents were traveling, I lived there. But when they were home, Dad would drive me to the Water House on week-ends and, the moment we rounded the bend along the ocean, he would toot the horn of his station wagon in rhythmic fashion to announce our arrival.

Grandma would open the doors and walk down the stairs, a vision in white. Over her flowered cotton house-dress she always wore a large baker's apron. Her hair, face, and apron were often covered in flour. "Come to Grandma," she sang. And as I hugged and kissed her, I still remember a flour cloud forming as I nestled into her arms.

That porch was a place of delicious memories.

When the doors opened we could smell the fresh tomato sauce cooking that she would use to smother her ravioli or—for what she called a healthy afternoon snack—green beans and potatoes swimming in the sauce. My younger sister's green bean memory is of bushels on the porch waiting for us to prepare so Grandma could "put them up," which meant preserving them in Mason jars. We would spend what seemed like forever sitting on the front porch as Grandpa would bring in the green beans. Our job was to break off the stems and snap them to fit into canning jars.

My sister, Debbie, remembers that Grandma's food always tasted better than food served anywhere else. "And once day, when Grandma asked me to go to the cellar for a jar of her homemade grape juice, I felt that I had discovered her cooking secret. I remember staring at rows of canning jars—long rows of colorful fruits and vegetables. And I remember thinking, 'To think this is all from Grandpa's garden. I stood there staring at the rows of what seemed like hundreds of jars until Grandma called to me, 'Did you find the grape juice.' Her words broke my trance."

We sat at the table for our green beans and potatoes. She brought out her small glasses with painted oranges and leaves and poured the regal purple liquid into each glass."

Thinking of the food at Grandma and Grandpa's house made for colorful images that paint a picture of happy memories. As we sat to eat, after saying the grace, Grandma would add: "You are blessed. Some children eat food from a can. Thanks to Grandpa, you children have food from God's good earth. Always be grateful for this."

Fireworks, flying horses, and frozen custard

Summer rituals and fireworks always take my breath away. Growing up Italian, we loved having any excuse for a celebration. One of my favorite times was gathering on the lawn at Grandma and Grandpa's house on the water to watch the fireworks. Then the next day we strolled along the boardwalk to a nearby amusement park where we indulged in frozen custard and rides on the flying horses. But Grandma always warned us, "Stay away from the mechanical fortune teller in the glass booth. That woman is trouble."

Although the amusement park was just several blocks away, Grandma did not like strangers and crowds. She was even more cautious on the Fourth of July weekend when she saw cars maneuvering the narrow road in front of the house. "They are not from around here," she would say. For that reason, she would invite family, friends and neighbors to sit on the large wrap-around porch or the lawn to view the amusement park's blossoming array of colors under the safety of her watchful eyes.

During the fireworks display, she would bring out her trays of biscotti and pass them around as if she was serving guests at a wedding. And after the finale of booming sounds, either Grandpa or my father led the singing of "Happy Birthday." Every year my father would say, "Can you believe that all these people came here for you?" My family would shower me with presents and I was led to believe that the fireworks were a gift from the neighbors for my birthday.

Despite Grandma's misgivings, we would head to the amusement park very early in the day. From the time I was a baby, my mother and aunts would take me for a boardwalk adventure. Grandma said one day, "Much as that place gives me the woollies, your mother looked forward to the frozen custard stand. Papa knew the owner, and when he saw you and my girls, he would open early for you. I knew they went there because you always came home with ice cream all over you."

What I also loved about that summer ritual was the ride on the flying horses. When my father caught the brass ring, before the music started, the operator would walk along the horses and tell everyone to sing "Happy Birthday" just for me.

In terms of happy memories, Grandma often reminded me of my favorite horse, a white stallion who I named Posies, because she had so many pretty flowers around her.

Whenever we returned from that park, Grandma would say, "I'll bet Posies was happy to see you. Flying horses are magical. They will always remember you and they will always give you a smile."

Circa 1944: a trip to the Savin Rock boardwalk.

Baked Stuffed Clams from "Nanny's Table"

Clamming, fried zucchini flowers, and love

Periwinkle snails, clams, and batter-fried zucchini flowers might seem like an odd combination, but in the world of Grandma and Grandpa, these spelled summer love. The front lawn of their house bordered a rock pile wall with a small dock. The back yard beyond the grape arbor was a huge garden of vegetables. On days when Grandpa would take us to gather periwinkles and go clamming, we knew that Gram would be in the garden picking zucchini flowers.

We loved clamming time with Grandpa. During low tide the sandbars were teaming with life. Before heading out Gram reminded us, "Now stay close to Papa."

And he answered, "Nancy, please, you teach them cooking. I teach them clamming."

We would then race to the beach stairs at the water's edge because at the end we knew we would find hundreds of periwinkles, tiny black snails hugging the giant rocks and dock pilings. When we had filled three hefty buckets Grandpa would let us sit on the dock while he carried the buckets to the kitchen pantry.

Then it was clamming and mud time. "When you see that water squirting, you know it's a clam," was Grandpa's mantra.

He used a tool to get to the clams, but we used our hands and small shovels. And each time we pulled up a clam, Grandpa's voice rang out, "Eh, bravo." But part of sandbar fun was to squish our feet in the cool, jet black mud where the clams nestled.

Once back home with overflowing buckets of clams, there Gram was smiling and waving her bar of Castile soap. "Into the outdoor shower you go." While we dried off and dressed under the grape arbor, she went to the kitchen to make us zucchini flowers dipped in egg, flour and milk—which turned crunchy in her huge black frying pan. After devouring the delicacy, we rested until dinner.

First course on clamming day dinner was the periwinkle challenge. After boiling them for two to three minutes, Grandpa carried a large plate to the table and gave us toothpicks to pull the meat from of the tiny shells and dip into hot butter. As we poked at the periwinkles, Grandma brought two more dishes to the table. Spaghetti and clams in broth as well as dishes of baked stuffed clams.

Our mother wrote up her stuffed clam recipe and included it in our family cookbook, *Nanny's Kitchen*.

STUFFED CLAM INGREDIENTS

2 -3 cloves chopped garlic

½ cup chopped onion

½ cup chopped Italian parsley

½ to 1 pound small scallops and fresh clams

Butter to taste

Lemon for garnish

COOKING PROCESS

Saute in a large frying pan over medium heat for about 5 minutes

Add ½ to 1 pound small scallops and chopped fresh clams

Smash or blend to a bread crumb consistency 1 ½ long packages of
    Ritz crackers

Add these to the saute mixture

A dash or two of white wine if the mixture is too dry

Fill a greased clam shell with a mound of the mixture

Finish each clam shell mound with a pat of butter and bake for about
    ½ hour at 375 degrees

Serve with lemon slices

*Circa 1947: Dad handing us presents from the window of the
station wagon. My sister, Lois, and I were in matching dresses
that our mother made for us.*

Biscotti for fabric: A happy trade off

To Grandma, looking fashionable was as simple as taking off the white baker's apron that usually hugged her pastel-colored house dress. It was only on Sunday, when she dressed for church in her navy-blue gabardine dress with the lace collar, that we could see her sense of style. When her daughters tried to take her shopping, she would say, "I'm not like Papa's mother, your *great a nonna*, who was always out and about. I'm here cooking and baking."

Nonetheless, Grandma appreciated fine cotton and linen and, to keep us looking fashionable, she became a barterer—her biscotti for the newest in fabric.

Our mother worked in the city at the telephone company, where she and her friends tried to dress according to fashion. They would shop on their lunch hour at Horowitz Bros., a fabric store with textiles, patterns, buttons and zippers. When our mother discovered that Angie, a saleswoman, lived near the Water House, she told her to simply knock on the door whenever she walked by and could smell Grandma's freshly baked biscotti.

Every few weeks, Angie would catch the aroma of Grandma's baking, and a predictable routine ensued. She would stand under the grape arbor and call out, "Nancy, are you in the kitchen? It's me. Angie." Grandma would lift the window frame and call out, "Angie, I was just thinking about you. Come in. The back door is open. You are just in time for some biscotti and demitasse."

On cue, Angie would say, "I don't want to bother you, but I did want you to know that we had some new fabrics. I think that your granddaughters will look adorable in this pattern if you and your girls have time to sew them some new dresses."

Then, seating herself at the table, she would say, "Now don't fuss. Just sit with me and we can talk." That was the sign that Angie was having company and wanted to bring home some biscotti.

Grandma kept Angie and her husband happy with sweets and, in exchange, Angie brought fabric swatches and sometimes even fabric remnants. On some Saturdays, our mother and her sisters would invite Angie to their sewing bee. They transformed the front parlor overlooking the water into a sewing room. There they spent the afternoon designing their own patterns, cutting and basting dresses, and then waiting for Grandma to "run them up" on her old Singer sewing machine on the second-floor balcony overlooking the parlor.

Angie was never as much fun as our aunts, but Grandma said it was because she had a difficult husband. "That's why I tell you all the time, be nice to everyone. You never know what troubles they carry in their hearts."

When the wandi became a family legend

Grandma took great pride in her cooking. Even though Grandpa worked at the pastry shop with his family, Grandma created delicacies that were just for her children and grandchildren. One of her prize creations consisted of paper-thin fried dough sprinkled with powdered sugar. These are often called *wandi*, traditionally shaped like wheels. However, Grandma fashioned hers into angels' wings for a combined celebration of July birthdays. Making them was time consuming and often took her a full day. These were handled with reverence.

When I young and living at their Water House, I would sit and watch Grandma mixing the batter of eggs, sugar, flour, baking powder and butter. She would then break the dough into sections and knead it. After letting me help roll the dough paper thin, Grandma carefully cut strips with a pastry wheel. Next, she fashioned them into wings and took them to her kitchen treasure, the black frying pan with boiling oil. She fried them for just about a minute on each side, before scooping them up with a slotted spatula and placing them onto long sheets of brown pastry paper for draining.

Then, on an afternoon in my sister's new Volkswagen Beetle, the wandi story changed forever. It was the day of the ladies' afternoon birthday party at our parents' home in a suburb about 15 minutes from the Water House. My sister Lois decided to show off her new white VW Beetle, and offered to pick up Grandma and her delicacies. In recalling the incident, she said, "What was I thinking? Did I really expect Grandma would love my bug as much as Dad's station wagon?" The challenge was space. Grandma was just over 4 feet tall and about as wide.

With our younger sister, she drove from the suburbs to the Water House. Debbie, who had been sitting in the front seat, got up, and carefully placed the wandi on the back seat, and then helped Grandma settle in front. Next, she had to squeeze behind Grandma and maneuver her way into that tiny space in the back seat. Mission accomplished, she flopped herself down.

Lois said, "All I could hear was a scream and a crunch." Debbie had landed on the angel wings.

Grandma was even more crushed than her cookies. Throughout the party, she kept repeating, "Can you believe that Debbie sat on my wandi? But don't say anything. I don't want her to feel bad. It wasn't her fault. The car was too small."

As soon as Grandpa came home that evening, Grandma practically wept as she told him the story—even before he had a minute to take off his suit jacket. Remembering her often repeated words of wisdom, "Never go to bed angry. Always end the day with a smile," Grandpa listened patiently. Told her that even crushed she made the world's best wandi. As she began to smile, suddenly he took hold of her and kissed her.

Grandpa could always bring a smile to Grandma's face.

*The boudoir doll, so popular during the Jazz Age, made a
popular comeback the 1950s.*

She crocheted dolly bed warmers and antimacassars

It was during a holiday visit to Cape Cod recently that we began to reminisce about Italian customs and remembrances.

Zia Contina, often in her pink chenille robe and matching hair curlers, loved her bed dolls with their rows upon rows of ruffles. Uncle Ronaldo called them "dust collectors."

When Grandma was not making antimacassars to protect her chairs from her Navy men, nephews who had pomade in their hair, she was crocheting outfits for dolls. You could often hear her say, "God gave these boys a good head of hair and what do they do? They slick it down with that Vaseline and mineral oil pomade. If I didn't have these antimacassars on the chairs, I would have to put a *moppina* under their heads. Just how do you think that would make them feel?"

Although she liked making antimacassars, the doll dresses gave her a chance to be creative. Unlike dolls for children, these were made for adult women.

We began a search for these dolls within the family. While everyone seemed to have a box in the attic filled with crocheted doilies that sat on the arms of chairs or antimacassars for the back of chairs, no one seemed to have saved the bed dolls.

However, in asking who in the family still owned one, we learned a bit about their history and significance. These were especially popular during the Roaring '20s when such dolls were dressed elaborately. Then during the late '40s, the dolls were often depicted in the detective series featuring Nick and Nora Charles, characters created by Dashiell Hammett in his novel *The Thin Man* and adapted for the movies.

Zia Contina, a longtime family friend, said that Grandma would crochet dresses and give the dolls as special gifts whenever she took a break from her kitchen and her baking. Advertisements for boudoir doll patterns began appearing in publications. But Grandma was as opposed to patterns as she was to recipes, saying: "What good is it if you can't create it yourself?"

Grandma liked making different designs with antimacassars and said that sometimes just adding rows of ruffles to skirts became tedious. It was then that she began to create dolls with bridal dresses, baby dolls with bonnets, and even costumes for summer and winter. Boudoir dolls could have movable arms and legs and eyes that even opened and closed. Or you could just buy a head to attach to a cloth body. For Grandma, there was just one choice: "If I'm going take the time to dress a doll, I want dolls in my house, not just a bag of heads."

A blessing lost and found

Grandma always had a house full of food ready to be turned into a scrumptious meal. The family house was on the water and she cooked enough to feed the Navy should sailors drop anchor at their dock. She liked to be prepared. When she knew that she was going to visit someone on the weekend, she would make her homemade ravioli, one of her pies, or her secret biscotti recipe.

However, when our sister from Massachusetts made a surprise visit one day with her new daughter, Grandma had nothing prepared. Despite concerns—as she said, "making a visit empty-handed"—we convinced her to come see the baby.

As happens with babies, the little princess was sound asleep when Grandma arrived. Nonetheless Gram was surrounded by nieces, nephews, and her own children and grandchildren. Everyone pitched in and brought their favorite dishes. Our mother draped a tablecloth on the picnic table and then set up smaller card tables that held enough food to share with the entire town.

There were classic dishes that we could always expect from relatives. Our mother made an antipasto, which in itself was a meal. On a large oval dish, she created a design of prosciutto, salami, pepperoni, hard cheeses and mozzarella, fresh tomatoes drizzled with olive oil, a variety of olives, roasted peppers and the traditional pickled vegetables.

Aunt Rose made her Jell-O squares. These were colored layers with a cream cheese filling in between. Aunt Chris always brought meatballs. Although they were sometimes a bit salty, we would each take one and say politely, "These look delicious."

Since it was a barbecue day, the grill was fired up for the *braciole*—tender thin slices of meat filled with chopped parsley, garlic, pignoli nuts and Parmesan cheese.

Grandma kept asking to see the baby. Although she had a peek, she wanted to hold her and hug her. We promised that as soon as it was dessert time, we would wake little Carrie.

As we started to eat, the "thanks for making this" became generous and plentiful. Suddenly something happened. Grandma's eyes began to water. "What's wrong?" we asked.

Grandma said, "You made me rush out in such a hurry that I came empty-handed. And now, I have missed out on the blessing. We are grateful to everyone who brought food. They were blessed. You give. And you receive."

We reassured her that she always gave and today it was her turn to receive. When we all posed for the photo with the little princess, Grandma took the baby's hand, smiled and said, "Yes, she is the blessing. It's good that I came here today."

*My sister, Lois, holding baby Carrie, Me, Grandma, Mother,
sister Debbie. (1971)*

Aunt Rose and our Mother were Biscotti twins
for holidays and weddings.

Best-ever under the grape arbor

The grape arbor at Gram and Grandpa's house was a welcome retreat at the end of the day. The rich royal-purple Concord grapes were plump and succulent. Grandpa's grapes became his wine, which he enjoyed every afternoon at 4 o'clock. While neighbors complained about the August heat, Grandma reminded us to think about what we loved most about the month. That was easy—sitting under the grape arbor watching them taste wine from the first jug of the season and thinking about Grandma's jams, Italian wine-dunking biscotti, and wine-laced tomato sauce.

While neighbors would sit on the porches looking at the still ocean, which seemed like a sea stuck in time, Gram would take us to the grape arbor. She would remind us of all the work that went into building the grape leaf canopy.

Each day she would find a different way to retell the story, from planting to putting in the posts that the vines hugged.

We would also spend hours under a giant weeping willow tree, where we played house, and parted the branches that became our door, to watch Grandpa tending the grape arbor. He explained to us that we had the most special of all grapes growing right in our yard. And Gram's Concord grape jam was a treasured gift.

She and Grandpa would sit under the arbor, taste the wine, and say always to each other, "Yes, this is by far the best." Then they would dip Italian biscuits shaped like small doughnuts into the wine. After a bite or two followed by another sip, Grandpa uttered a loud, "Ah bravo. Nancy, this is like wine and food from the old country."

One day we asked Gram, "Does it really get better each year?"

Gram answered, "If Papa thinks this is the best year, and it makes him happy to believe it, then 'yes' this is best wine ever. When you get married remember that sometimes it is easier to say 'yes' and then just believe. Papa works so hard to tend to those grapes and it takes so many steps to make the wine that the flavor brings joy to him. Who knows? Maybe this wine is the best ever."

That afternoon she asked with a twinkle in her sapphire shining eyes, "Are these the best ever biscotti that I have made for you?" It's a question that our mother and Aunt Rose asked after each tray of biscotti they made for weddings and family parties. And the answer was always, "Yes, these are the best ever."

BISCOTTI INGREDIENTS

8 tablespoons (1 stick) unsalted butter

½ cup sugar

2 egg yolks

1 cup milk

Grated lemon zest from one lemon

2 teaspoons baking powder

¾ cup sesame seeds (For pepper biscotti substitute cracked pepper for sesame seeds)

COOKING PROCESS

In a large bowl, beat the butter and sugar together until combined

Beat in the yolk, milk and zest. (Mixture will look as if it is curdled–do not panic)

Sift the flour with the baking powder, mixing until the dough comes together in a ball

Cover and refrigerate for at least one hour or up to one day to make the dough easy to handle

Preheat over to 375 degrees

Grease two large baking sheets and bake until lightly brown on each side

Our parents Engagement Photo 1941

Nights of falling stars and love

We grew up believing that meteorite showers were gifts from the heavens. For each star that fell into the arms of Mother Earth, we wished for love and kisses from our Prince Charming. Stars always glistened from the wrap-around porch at Gram and Grandpa's, which sat at the water's edge. From there we could see miles of ocean and sky while waiting for the magical stars to arrive. Nights of falling stars were a ritual: Ravioli dinner, greens, and gobs of gelato.

Although the house was filled with rooms, winding staircases, and even a widow's walk, Grandma lived in her kitchen which overlooked the grape arbor and the vegetable gardens. Her jolly body and print dresses were always covered by a large white baker's apron that matched her hair—almost always dusted with flour as she brushed wisps from her face.

On nights of falling stars we camped on the porch, fell asleep, and our grandparents would wake us when the star shower began. On those nights we would talk about our wishes and dreams. The first time we told them about a Prince Charming for each of us, being a practical man Grandpa spoke up. He put down his cigar, looked at us intently and said, "When you marry, he should be a kind man with a good job. And, if he is Italian—ah Bravo. Bravo."

Then Gram added that he should want at least four children and take us to church each Sunday even if he did not go inside. When she was rolling out dough to make her ravioli one day, we asked her if her falling star wishes all came true. She put her rolling pin aside, wiped the flour from her hands onto her apron, sat with us and smiled.

"Sometimes you need to pretend that everything is all right with your husband. When Papa comes home bellowing, I slip up the back stairs and go to my sewing room. Then I imagine that when I come downstairs, he will be my Prince Charming. By then he is on the porch with his cigar.

"Instead of complaining about the smell, I kiss him and say, 'I'm happy you are home, Anthony.' He softens and becomes my prince," she said. "Sometimes, I don't even go to the sewing room, I just kiss him when he walks in and act as if I didn't hear his roar."

Then Gram added, "When you know your husband is having a bad day, you are going to expect an old grump to walk in the house. Instead see him as your prince. Give him a big hug and a kiss and see how love wins out."

III. FALL AND FOREVER MEMORIES

Circa 1945: Grandpa was proud of his finocchio.

Grandpa's garden was his other love

As the harvest moon implies, September marked the time when Grandpa would be bringing in the last of the vegetables from the garden. And for Grandma, her canning season would begin. "Even though I put up all these vegetables for the winter, just look at the treasure you girls have—you eat fresh from the back yard every day."

This was the season when Grandpa loved showing off his fennel plants, *finocchio* and a prize *cucuzza*. An Italian squash known to grow up to three feet long, *cucuzza* became a key ingredient for a month of meals.

Grandpa was so proud of his *finocchio*, that he would bring them to some of the merchants in town near the family pastry shop. With a texture similar to celery and an anise taste, we would have them sliced thin for munching between courses at dinner or slivered into a salad to accompany a *cucuzza* dish.

My younger sister just wrote me of their trip to a roadside stand. "Our intention was to pick up fresh peppers, but lo and behold they were selling *cucuzza*. I had to buy a 3-foot-long squash to make stuffed canoes, and Gramma Water Stew. Can't you just taste the *cucuzza*, onions, garlic, carrots, fresh lima beans, and tomatoes?"

"Not only could I conjure up the taste, I can still see Grandma dipping her long ladle into the deep soup pan, then pouring the sweet-tasting stew onto a thick frizelle at the bottom of a bowl to seep in the juices. Then at the table there would be a shaved stack of Parmesan cheese to top off the meal," writes Debbie.

My sister remarked, after making it in her own kitchen, "All we needed was a glass of Gram's homemade grape juice and it would be like having her standing there, smiling, and saying, '*Mangia*.'"

While Grandma and all of us savored the stew, Grandpa's favorite was the stuffed *cucuzza*. After scooping out the squash, Grandma would dice a yellow onion and mix it with diced Roma tomatoes, fresh garlic, parsley, and basil and mix it together with *cucuzza*.

Then she would add bread stuffing, usually day-old crusted bread that she soaked in water. She mixed this together with diced mozzarella and an egg and stuffed the canoes. Before baking she topped the dish with some fresh tomato sauce and Parmesan cheese. While it baked, it seemed as if the entire neighborhood had the aroma of her little village in Italy.

When we would sit to eat, Grandpa would pinch her cheek and say, "Eh Brava." She would teasingly push away his hand, then hold it and say, "Now we give thanks."

The Fiorentina pears, a tray of cookies, and a bridal bag

Grandma spoke of "Papa's pears" with reverence. The fruit trees that lined the walkway to Grandpa's garden created a canopy that overheard family secrets and stories including our favorite—the pears for newlyweds. Grandma said that in her Italian village when young people married and moved from the farms "to set up house," her mother would bring them a basket of pears. Since pear trees live for 250 years, these were wishes for a long, happy life together.

In this country, Gram kept up the spirit of tradition. Each fall she lined the pantry with jars for her pears in brandy. She made up a simple mixture of boiled sugar to which she added bay leaves and brandy and then the cored and sliced pears.

Each year at pear time, soft-spoken Gram would raise her voice.

"Anthony, Anthony," she would call out. "That brother of yours was back in my pantry again. He knew I was making the pears and look at how much brandy he drank. I'm telling you, it's time to talk with him."

"Aspetta, my little sweetheart. I bought more brandy just for you."

Grandpa's little sweetheart was about 4 feet 10 inches tall and just as wide. They would kiss. She would smile then sigh. "Imagine he drinks the newlyweds' brandy for their pears of long life."

Grandma believed "Papa's pears" were descendants of the Fiorentina pears, which her mother had received as a gift from relatives in Umbria, about three hours from their village in the Avellino region. The Fiorentina pear tree is often depicted in Renaissance paintings.

Since family weddings took place in the summertime, Grandma and Grandpa waited until the fall to visit newlyweds at their home. She packed jars of pears in a large basket and on top of the jars rested a small tray of her biscotti sprinkled with sugar-coated almonds and silver stands of tinsel—a miniature of their wedding tray.

At Italian weddings newlyweds passed a large tray of cookies to guests. The bride always had a drawstring satin pouch swinging from her wrist. When relatives took the cookies, they handed the bride an envelope with cash, saying, "Put this in your bag. A little something to help you set up house."

Immediately after the exchange of cookies and envelopes, Gram nudged Grandpa. On cue, he stood up, lifted his wine glass and began his toast. "Here's to the bride and the groom. I want you both to look around at all of your family. My wife just reminded me to tell you that marriage is for richer, for poorer. Even on days when you feel poor, remember this moment. Here you have surrounding you the riches of family. *Salute.*"

Pears for newlyweds to wish them a long life together.

Little Italy Italian Feast. courtesy of Wikipedia.

Feast of San Gennaro and the feast of family

Our grandmother disliked crowds, even those that gathered to honor the saints. When September's "*la festa de San Gennaro*" approached—a large Italian street festival of music, games and food—Gram planned a gathering of some 30 relatives for cooking, eating, playing bocce and building sand castles. She said we could not attend the feasts until we were tall enough to see over the heads of the crowd. The city feast that began in Naples was transported to Italian-American neighborhoods and featured the saint's statue being carried through the streets.

At our house, there was no saint to be lifted onto men's shoulders, just buckets of sand from under the dock to our front lawn so that we could build our sand village. While the men gathered sand, we went with aunts and cousins to the gardens to pick the last of the escarole, cabbage and kale to make "minestra," a greens and beans staple for the first September chill.

As Gram and our aunts cooked, Grandpa and the men prepared the bocce court, a patch of soil about 16 feet long by about 8 feet wide. With balls made of metal, the game was like bowling without the pins.

When the sun began to set over the water, Grandpa moved his Victrola (a record player that had to be cranked up) to the side porch so we could listen to Italian music from his 78 RPM records. Then he hung colored Christmas lights over the grape arbor saying: "Now it looks like the Italian feast."

Once we all took our place at the picnic tables, we bowed our heads as he thanked God for family and food. Then Grandma and our aunts came along to place a large frizelle in everyone's dish. The thick crusty slice of Italian bread seemed lonely until it was smothered by a hefty ladle of "minestra." Later the tables were cleared for gobs of homemade gelato as Grandpa and the men turned on the Christmas lights over the bocce court. Then they poured themselves wine and raised their glasses, saying "*Salute*."

We all moved onto the porch to watch and cheer on the teams. Smiling from her rocker, Gram nodded her head contentedly. Then she said, "If all those people at the city festival knew about this day, they would wish they could be here. If you went to the city, you would have missed all of this. Sometimes you will have wishes that may not come true. Instead of pouting, create a better memory. Look around you. We have colored lights, good food, relatives and music.

"Today while the city celebrates San Gennaro, we are celebrating the feast of food and family."

After the fig tree was snug in the ground

There is a painting by Sandra Bierman, "The Planting," which portrays a woman on her knees with her hands almost cuddling a seedling tree. It was with similar reverence that Grandpa treated his fig tree, raised from a cutting he brought from the old country. Grandma said, "That fig tree, I'm telling you, he takes care of it just like it was a pet."

Figs from Grandpa's tree were sweet and succulent because, he said, "I bury her each year. This climate here is cold. She needs to be protected. In the ground, the good earth keeps her warm and safe. That's why I take your grandmother to Florida each year—for the warmth."

In truth, Grandma was never happy about going to Florida to stay with her in-laws. We do not have a single picture of her smiling under a palm tree. Why did she go? "If it makes him happy, what's to say?" she would shrug. "He works hard."

Although there was a major ritual in the springtime when Grandpa and his brothers unearthed the tree, preparing to bury the tree was something that Grandpa did with just one of his brothers. Grandpa would start digging the trench before the ground hardened but was careful to protect the roots of the tree. Then just after Halloween, he would prune the branches. The next day one of his brothers came by to hold the tree upright while he cut some roots. Once my youngest sister and cousins came by and Grandpa let them help. They felt so proud when he said, "I couldn't have done this without you."

Then of course, Grandma would come to witness the moment in which the tree was wrapped, tied with rope, put into the ground, and covered with leaves. Then came a tarp and some boards before the men dragged a big wooden rowboat over the shallow ditch for further protection.

By now Grandma would have slipped away to the kitchen to brew the demitasse, put out a bottle of anisette, and arrange her biscotti on a tray. The two men would walk in smiling. Then, pinching her cheek, Grandpa would say,

"Nancy, she's safe in the ground. Now, we leave for Florida and come back before the election."

Grandpa liked to return home by the first of November for two reasons. He wanted to be involved in the elections. But also, in Europe, All Souls Day is a serious time to visit the graveside of one's relatives. After burying the tree, Grandpa would make a sign of the cross, look to the heavens, a say, "Momma, *grazie*." Then, on All Soul's Day, because his mother was buried in the old country, he would sit by the rowboat where the fig tree was buried and simply pray the Rosary. His black beads were always in his pocket.

While Grandpa loved the Florida sun with his family,
Grandma rarely smiled while she was there.

Pasta and Anchovies

Grandma's politics and puttanesca

Because she never learned to read in English, Grandma appeared to be disinterested in politics. Nonetheless, politicians frequently stopped by for her Friday night Puttanesca, an Italian dish of spaghetti, anchovies, olives and capers. During election season, she made this meal in huge vats. On Saturday, neighbors would visit to ask her opinions. Little thoughts and gestures from Grandma could set people thinking in a voters' world that relied more on gossip than facts.

Despite backroom politics—as well as heated discussions at men's private Italian clubs—women would pry Gram for inside information. Gram would say, "We never know what goes on behind closed doors." And if she did not answer in words, it was never a good sign when she tilted her head, shrugged her shoulders, and threw up her hands.

During one closely watched race, neighbors pushed her for an answer as to her favorite candidate. She smiled and said, "You know I don't take sides. They are both good men. They often sit at my table. But only one brings his wife—and even his mother."

"Ahh, his mother? That tells us everything," they nodded.

After every election, Grandma would receive a large basket of fall fruit and flowers from the winning candidate. Many years later, Grandma's influence was still talked about. When I returned to New Haven from New York, where I had been studying, I became involved in a medical center expansion project. The center, focusing on drug treatment research, was stalled by "not in my backyard" activists.

At a crucial meeting of politicians and physicians, when the mayor arrived—even before we introduced ourselves—he looked at me and said, "Little lady, do you have a family recipe for spaghetti and anchovies from your grandmother, Nancy? You look just like her."

Before answering, he told the story of political Puttanesca. "Gentleman, if you were running for office some years back, you simply had to knock on the door of Nancy and Anthony and join the family. There was always room for one more."

He added: "Our family was another story. We were not in politics back then. We had very little money. But every Friday night, her Grandma sent over a pot of spaghetti and anchovies and we feasted." Then he raised his eyes to the heavens and said, "Nancy, thank you, we are going to make the new center a reality—the Puttanesca center."

Amid laughter and applause, he turned to me and said, "I have just one request—her recipe."

The mayor was given the recipe. The center was built. And on that day, years later, Gram's often repeated words rang true: "Give to others and goodness will come back to you."

PUTTANESCA INGREDIENTS

8 cloves garlic

3 oz olive oil

3 oz large capers

5 oz green olives with pimentos

6 oz pitted black olives Ingredients:

A handful of hot cherry peppers

4 cans anchovies

1 tablespoon of pesto

1 tablespoon of margarine

2 generous pinches of rosemary

¼ cup of fresh flat Italian parsley

2—3 pounds of Capellini or Angel Hair pasta

COOKING PROCESS

Sauté the peeled and finely chopped garlic clove in hot oil until browned

Add the olives, chopped, and the chopped cherry peppers

Cook together over medium heat for a few minutes and then add the
anchovies, pesto, rosemary, and chopped parsley

Cook the pasta according to taste

Drain leaving a little water in the pan

Mother and me — Spring 1944

Grandma's olive oil secret to beautiful skin and a long life

Grandma's Puttanesca was laden with olive oil. And she began slathering herself with it when she knew she was going to Florida. She was convinced that the sun would dry out her skin. When she returned she took the can from under the sink and began her ritual. It was a ritual that our mother believed kept her looking young—olive oil and her cooking.

Our mother loved visiting new physicians, so she could entertain them with stories of why she looked so young at 90 years of age. "I live like my mother and father did by eating fresh vegetables, beans, and cooking with pure olive oil. I still make the escarole and beans the way my mother taught us, with a little garlic and a bit of prosciutto."

What she never did admit, however, was keeping the can of olive oil under the sink—as did her mother. It had to be nearby so that you could pour a bit in your hands and then rub it into your face to keep away the wrinkles.

The olive oil that remained after cooking was poured into a coffee can and rested on the counter. It was covered with a with a piece of wax paper so throughout the day the golden liquid was ready for her thick black frying pan. She used it for frying garlic to a light golden brown, which became the basis for all of her soups and tomato sauces. That same pan also welcomed her eggplant slices dipped in batter, her herb-infused sausage, peppers, and onions, as well as zucchini flowers.

"Grandma, why do you strain oil into a coffee can," I asked one day.

With a look of surprise, she answered: "So I can reuse it. It is full of good flavors. That's Grandma's cooking secret."

There was no dishwasher in the house and so everything was washed and rinsed by hand except for the black frying pan. You wiped it with piece of cloth that was as thin as cheesecloth. Grandma did not like using paper napkins on her frying pan because she knew that her own "pan clothes" were soaked and washed in Castile soap for four hours.

Midday she would say, "Now you can take them out and hang them on the line. Be sure they are not in the shade because I want them to have a sun-kissed scent."

Grandma believed that the secret to beautiful skin was under her sink—her can of olive oil. My mother and her sisters used it. And because Grandma was suspicious of oils made just for babies—I, too, was raised with the secret. I'm sure I was the only baby in the neighborhood who smelled like a salad.

Great a Nonna's clash with the padre

In my great *nonna*'s day, when the 90-year-old widow was seen on the arm of a younger man, the padre warned that she could be denied a church burial. Our older relatives were outraged since priests in Italy were long rumored to have their own young companions.

By age 104, the health of Zia Dolce—as great *nonna* was called—began to fail. Her daughter-in-law, my Gram, talked about it with Gram's philandering brother, Albertino. He vowed to travel to the old country "to make things right." We can still hear his wife, Aunt Georgia: "This is another excuse for you to go charm those village girls with your smiles and your roses. The woman who is dying is the mother of your aunt's husband. And her husband, Zio Pasquale, died 10 years ago."

He said, "Georgia, out of respect for the fathers in this family, I need to see that Zia Dolce is buried next to her husband."

Gram raised her eyebrows, but, thinking of her husband, she whispered, "It will make Papa happy."

So, Uncle Albertino traveled to a hillside village in Campania. After heading straight to the church, he wrote, saying, "The priest defended the Commandments too vigorously. My mission begins."

With his smile and armloads of flowers he chatted with the villagers who knew Zia Dolce. Eventually, he attracted a saucy gal who said "no" to the flowers, but happily offered to sit with him and share some vino at a small café.

It was only after her returned home that I learned the story. There was a room above the parlor. And if you scrunched under Grandma's sewing machine, no one could see you. But you could hear every word said in the parlor.

Overhearing him re-enact the story to his brothers, it seems that many drinks, secrets and kisses later, he dramatically rose to his feet. Then he cried out to the heavens: "Mamma mia. I will surely be punished for coveting the padre's *comare*. I am breaking one of the commandments of God."

And that is how he got to the truth. She just giggled, "No. I'm not the one. It's the girl from San Gregorio Magno. We call her Anna Maria de Tarantella because she leads the dance to music from the zampogna" (Italian bagpipes).

Uncle Albertino returned to the padre asking that he visit Zia, forgive her, and honor her husband—father of their 12 children—by burying her next to Zio Pasquale in the church cemetery. The padre protested, "She does not believe that she and Tonio are living in sin."

Handing him a funeral donation, he said, "If your conscience and the church forbid this, maybe Zia can be buried next to Anna Maria de Tarantella."

Within the next few weeks, my great *nonna*'s funeral was celebrated at the tiny parish church. Her final resting place, next to her husband, was covered with flowers. Tonio, her 80-ish grief-stricken companion, was consoled by the village widows. And Uncle Albertino, pleased that he brought respect to a good husband and father, treated himself to an extra week in the arms of the woman who helped him "to make things right."

A small church in the region

Lois's Recreation of Grandma's Cutlets

A tale of diamonds, love, lasagna, and cutlets

Grandma and Grandpa kept the Christmas decorations up until well past the time when the three wise men were expected to arrive. And it was always during the first week of the New Year that Zia Agatha and Uncle Federico would visit, arms filled with pastry for a second Christmas feast. Even though Grandpa ran the pastry shop with his sister Agatha, Gram was always miffed when someone else brought pastry into her home.

After rounds of kisses, to continue the ritual even in the most frigid weather, Federico and Grandpa would go off to the porch to smoke their cigars. Since Gram didn't want Zia in her kitchen, she would hand her the salt and pepper shakers to put on the table and then said, "Zia, everything is done. Come sit by the fire."

Zia took her cue to regale us with countless tales of her whirlwind courtship in the old country. Gram's twinkling blue eyes would begin their roll.

Great Zia Agatha prided herself on being married forever and wore a diamond on each finger as proof of Federico's love for her. Gram said that the diamonds were gifts from Federico because he took so many trips to Naples to breathe the good Italian air into his lungs, to restore his soul, and to renew his strength. What Zia called "his exercise" came from a bevy of younger women in his native village.

We had always suspected that Federico was a ladies' man because of whispers and looks that other relatives had shared about his *comares*. On this particular Sunday, Aunt Georgia stopped by to complain about her philandering husband, the younger brother of Zia and Grandpa. Unlike his plump siblings, her husband was tall, thin, and always dressed in a white pin-striped suit, black shirt, and wore black patent leather shoes with spats.

Zia barely acknowledged Georgia and so continued her tale of Federico's love. That's when Zia's sister-in-law dared to say, "Zia, please. He is as bad your brother, my husband"

Zia let out a loud wail and grabbed her heart and the massive diamond pin resting on her hefty breasts. Gram took advantage of the drama to slip away. Then Zia reached into her dress for her lace handkerchief, dabbed at her eyes filling with tears and sobbed, "Federico. My Federico. He is my one and only love. Look at my diamonds."

With that, Grandma opened the French doors separating the dining room and living room. Setting down a large antipasto she motioned to us: "Tell Papa and Federico to come in. I cooked all day. I want to bring out the lasagna and chicken cutlets. Everyone—to the table."

SAUCE FOR CUTLETS INGREDIENTS
One dozen plum tomatoes
4 cloves of garlic
Fresh basil to taste

COOKING PROCESS
Boil plum tomatoes slightly to remove the skin
Set aside
Fry garlic slices until golden brown
Mix the skinned tomatoes into the pan, lightly so chunks will remain
Add a slight bit of water
Pour over the cutlets[1]
Top with fresh basil and bake

---

1   Choose any recipe that your like to prepare the cutlets. Top with a slice
of mozzarella. Then pour over them Grandma's sauce.

A family birthday in the mid-80s

Our Grandma's candy drawer of treats

Grandma loved a good party. She thrived preparing for Sunday dinners because to her, each Sunday meal was a party. Also, the Water House was so large that most birthdays were held there. The one party that Grandma seemed to brush off was her own birthday. "I don't even have a birth certificate," she would say. "How do we know when I was born?" Nonetheless, every January, Grandpa planned a party highlighted by an Italian cream and rum layer cake topped with a dozen sugar roses and the delicately formed words, "Happy Birthday, Nancy."

In looking at family photos, I was reminded that when Grandma could no longer host the family gatherings, our mother and her sisters took turns. The joy Grandma missed in cooking, she experienced in opening her birthday gifts.

While she always saved personal presents for herself, the candies that she would request were for her gift drawer. Italian confetti candies, shaped like a dime with a sugar shell and chocolate inside, came in pastel shades. Another favorite were sugar-coated almonds which, at weddings, were often sprinkled within a tray of biscotti that the bride and groom would pass around to each guest.

And, of course, Grandma liked to have boxes of Torrone, honey nougat candy with almonds or pistachios. She liked the little boxes because each had an image of a historic Italian figure. She said that her two favorites were Ippolita, first wife of the Duke of Calabria, who later reigned as King Alfonso II of Naples, and Ferrante Gonzaga, who defended Naples—"considered the old country"—against an invasion in the 1500s.

Grandma's gift drawer also had a flavored sugar confection made in Italy. These after dinner mints were called "Leone. Violet. For Spring Lovers."

For a few weeks after her birthday, she would pile the candies she had been given into a large orange iridescent Tiffany bowl on the dining room table.

Eventually, she would take them to the bottom drawer of a tall mahogany bureau with a carved Stuart rose design.

The drawer was always filled with sweets and crocheted handkerchiefs in an array of colors tucked inside a silk pouch. Whenever you came to visit Grandma unexpectedly and she did not have fresh biscotti ready for you to take home, she led you to the bureau of sweets. Opening the candy drawer, she would say, "Help yourself. These are gifts from my children for me to give to you to take home."

Her often repeated words to us: "You never go to anyone's house empty-handed. And you never let anyone leave your house empty-handed. Even if they do not bring you a gift, you give a gift to them. It's what you are supposed to do, it's a blessing."

An attic full of treasures

When Grandma would say to us, "Take this up to the attic," she was asking us to visit a treasure house of memories. The attic at the big house on the water had large leather trunks, all carefully labeled with the names of each of her children. There was also a trunk labeled "Pa and Ma" that contained mementos ranging from First Communion prayer books to wedding invitations.

As with her own mother, our Mother was a "saver." In addition to the trunk that Grandma kept with her children's names, our Mother started a trunk of her own labeled with her married name. We were amazed that some 40 years later we found this trunk, nearly intact, full of memories.

We discovered items from our parents' wedding invitation requesting "the honor of your presence on Saturday morning, September twelfth" to the invitation to attend my first birthday party. There were postcards from our father who was in the Army Air Force and even a postcard from her parents who wrote from Florida in 1949.

"Hello My Dear Ones. We are fine and hope you can say the same. We had a very good day at the beach. From dear Pa and Ma."

Even when our parents moved to their own apartment, Mother continued collecting photos and postcards, which now live in my sister's attic. In addition to photos of children, birthdays, family outings and days at the beach, these became filled with photos from our parents' travels. One of our favorites is an anniversary photo of them taken during their stay at the Fontainebleau in Miami Beach, where our dad, Vincent, was sound consultant to Frank Sinatra.

He became well-known in engineering circles for creating the concept of "sound without a shell," which made it possible for celebrity musicians to perform at the Yale Bowl in New Haven, Connecticut. Although he and our Mother always had front-row guest seats for these concerts, Grandma would not leave the house to be in a crowd. However, she did love to hear the behind-the-scenes stories and collect concert programs.

Oftentimes, the following day, a neighbor or two would stop by and say, "Tell us about the concert." Then, speaking as if she had been there herself, Grandma would place a program on the table and begin: "What I am going to tell you, you won't read in the papers."

She would brew her demitasse, take out a tray of biscotti, and with her neighbors, she would sit in the living room and enjoy the afternoon.

*Our parents celebrating their anniversary
at the Fountainbleau in Miami.*

Grandma and Grandpa, 1972

Grandma's pajama party

We slept over at Grandma's house last night. It was right after Grandpa's wake. She thought we were having a pajama party. Our arrival allowed her to step back in time to a place of granddaughters' visiting to enjoy her cooking and spend a weekend at the beach. Grandma loved making us a breakfast of her pancakes, one-inch think.

"This is a secret recipe from the old country," she would smile. Grandma did not attend the wake. She had said her good-byes to Grandpa two years earlier after he suffered a stroke, was sent to a nursing home, and there he remained until his death.

For many months after our little sister was born, we spent weekends at what cousins called "The Water House." As soon as our father came home from work, our mother would pack us into the back of his station wagon, with the wooden panels, and our excursion would begin. He listened to music from a scratchy sounding radio while my sister and I bickered in the back seat. I was nearly 10 and she was 6 years old.

There were miles of water along the road between where we lived and where Grandma and Grandpa lived. After what seemed like an endless drive, we would come around a bend and a stretch of large homes, facing the water, came into view. Dad would start beeping his horn in a rhythmic pattern. The first house we saw was the Castle House with its bright red and white turrets. Next to that was the dark green and yellow Water House with its wrap-around porch, large pillars and a widow's walk at the very top. When Grandma heard the beeping, she would come to the porch to greet us.

As we pulled into the driveway, she was there waving to us. Grandma was an awesome size at four feet tall plus and maybe even four feet wide. Her eyes twinkled blue and her hair shone a pure white, mostly from the baking flour that forever dusted her.

While dad put our bags on the porch we ran to her, one on each side. Then as we hugged, we stretched our arms around her until our fingers touched, and we nestled into her comfort.

Once at Grandma and Grandpa's we were safe from listening to the new baby's crying. Here we were lulled to sleep by sounds of the sea, from waves ebbing and flowing to fog horns moaning. And on stormy nights, when waves crashed against the dock and thunder roared, Grandma assured us, "It's just the sea fairies playing bocce ball. They need to have some fun, too."

The next morning our cousins, who lived about six streets over, would come by before sunrise.

Grandpa would take us fishing from the dock at high tide. And at low tide we would gather periwinkles or go clamming. On days when Grandpa took us to the beach, we knew that Gram would be in the garden picking zucchini flowers to batter and fry for an afternoon treat. Or she might be baking us a batch of her biscotti.

After Grandpa's stroke, Grandma went to the nursing home to see him. "He didn't look like himself. That's not Papa," she said. And from that day on, she convinced herself that he was on a long fishing trip. She would even go to the widow's walk and look out over the water waiting for his return.

When my sister and I arrived at the wake, having traveled there from New York, our mother looked over and saw us. But she did not leave her spot where she was sitting with her sisters off to the side of the casket. With Grandma not there, she was at the helm. She was clearly in command in her black Givenchy suit, white blouse and a little black ribbon tie at her neck. She could have asked anything of us that night and we could not have refused.

But "Sleep at the Water House? We just came here from the train. Why?" we asked.

"It's known as turns," she said. "It's your turn. You two choose to move away. All this time, those of us left alone here have spent nights with Grandma, who never liked the housekeepers we hired to look after her. But she refused to live with any of us, insisting that she had to be there when Papa came home."

Nearly 12 years had passed since our last sleepover. Suddenly it felt strange. We knew that Grandma was having problems with her memory. They called it "hardening of the arteries."

At 9 PM, the wake for Grandpa ended. Mother told us that in the morning the funeral procession would drive to the house and pause so Grandpa could pass by his home and beloved ocean.

Then she added, "But the funeral car will park in front for you. So, don't be late. It will be there promptly at 8:30 AM and then we will go right to the church."

After the wake, our cousins drove us from the funeral parlor to the Water House. It was a long ride along the ocean. We were transfixed by the blackness of the water. We remembered that it sometimes reflected streams of moonbeams, sometimes ominous clouds, sometimes just a hazy fog. Tonight, the water rippled. The buoys clanked their tin sounding bells and the fog horn moaned, almost as if they were saddened.

When we arrived at the house, the latest in an endless stream of housekeepers brought Grandma to greet us.

"Guess what?" we announced the minute we saw her. "We're sleeping over tonight, and we promise to be good." She looked at us and, as if she was trying to catch her breath, she traveled back in time.

"Oh, really? And who says you're invited? I don't know if a sick old lady like me can handle a pair of troublemakers like you. By the time all these people leave my house, I'm going to be tired. So, you better not cause any commotion," she smiled. She outstretched her arms. Then with one of us on each side, we hugged her until our fingers touched.

"What are all these people doing in my house bringing food?" she asked.

"Grandma there will be a lot of people here after the funeral tomorrow. These are all of your neighbors trying to be helpful."

As people began to leave, whenever someone said, "We are very sorry," Grandma replied, "He's been away a long time."

When we were alone with her, Grandma didn't give us a chance to talk about the people in her home, the wake, or the funeral. She did say, however, "I like people around. I just didn't know the people here tonight.

You know I loved when your mother had 'a time' here. She would bring all the girls from the telephone company over for a beach party. There were people everywhere, on the wrap-around porch and the entry foyer with its window seats."

Talking almost non-stop, finally Grandma took a breath and said, "I can see that you two don't eat right. Look at you, just skin and bones. You should stay with me. I'll get you looking healthy again."

Grandma, who had been suffering from bouts of depression, had become manic. She just kept on talking and led us to the master bedroom where she was delighting in rummaging through her drawers to find something for us to wear. The gunny sack fashion show began. Gram kept pulling nightgowns and bed jackets from her drawers saying, "Try this one and come show me."

We could have wrapped the two of us in one of her nightgowns, but we kept trying them on because she was enjoying each moment. We knew we should have talked with her about the funeral, but the time never seemed right. Finally, with a heap of nightgowns on her bed, she said, "Let's all sleep in the floating room; it was always your favorite."

Gram never slept anywhere other than the bed that she and Grandpa shared for years. And tonight, she led us to the room that looked as if it was suspended from the staircase on the side facing the parlor. It continued into a bedroom that had a strange way of jutting out onto a second story balcony. With the doors open, it looked as if you were floating on the sea. Funny how just hours before we were scrunching up our noses and saying, "Sleep over at Gram's? Why?" And now we three were plumped onto the huge bed, with Grandma in the center. As when we were children, the sea sounds carried us into dreamland.

The next morning, there were no cousins to run with us to the beach before sunrise. But Grandma had awakened early. As we made our way down the long staircase, we could see her sitting silently in the kitchen. We went to her and gave her a morning hug. She was not wearing one of her usual pink or pale blue housedresses with a white apron. Instead she was dressed in black.

"Grandma are you coming with us today?" we asked.

She didn't answer. She stood up and poured each of us a cup of demitasse.

Then as in our childhood, Grandma reminded us: "Well, you two were good girls for a change. You can come back next week. I'll tell your mother that you behaved yourselves." She walked into the parlor, looked out the side window and asked: "Is your father picking you up? We'll sit in the parlor and listen for him to start beeping the horn."

Whenever he picked us up, as soon as Grandma heard him beeping the horn, she would roll her eyes and say, "Thank God he's here." Then giving us a hug, she would add, "Good bye. Good riddance. And don't come back no more... not till next week."

But on that day of the funeral no sounds signaled the time for our departure. Only an ominous feeling told us that the mourning procession was arriving. We stood up. But before we could hug and kiss Grandma, she was already on the porch. We watched her as she stood silently overlooking the water. When the car for us pulled to the front of the house, she gasped. Her eyes watered. We held her tightly.

"Why?" she asked in a faint whisper. "Why?"

Damn black limousine. It spoiled Grandma's pajama party.

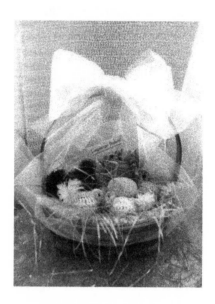

We left some of the crochet egg warmers
she made for us in her casket.

Grandma's funeral celebration of singing granddaughters

How we grandchildren came together to sing at Grandma's funeral remains a bit of a mystery. In thinking about Grandpa's funeral, we were a bit disconcerted. It seemed strangely impersonal. We wanted Grandma's send-off to be special, from her wake to her funeral. Grandma loved to crochet and we all had her gifts of tiny stockings for the Christmas tree or baby chick egg warmers for Easter. As we thought about her gifts to us, we decided to each bring a memento and place it with her in the casket.

Suddenly someone had a thought that was considered outrageous. Instead of wrapping rosary beads around her hands, we would have her holding knitting needles with a ball of yarn close-by.

Our mother was a bit concerned. What would the good nuns say when they arrived? But we did not spend too much time worrying because we had to get to a rehearsal. I found hymns that I knew she loved—and these same hymns we sang at our own mother's funeral. And it seemed quite simple. There was just one glitch, whenever we would start to sing, one of us would burst into tears.

A neighbor came to the rescue in the image of Fr. Guido Sarducci, a chain-smoking priest from "Saturday Night Live." With his wide brimmed monk's hat, he would offer music specials. His routine rarely varied. "Ladies and the gentlemen. I have here for $2.99 the music or for $4.99 the tape. Just send the money to the place on your screen."

Our neighbor came in one evening as we tried to rehearse and cry at the same time. Donning a monk's hat, she walked in saying, "*Ladies and the Gentle-men here. We havea for you thisa night the granda children. Justa the girls because the boys, they are gonna carry, you know, the casket. The girls are gonna sing the hymns for their Granna Mother's funeral. So take it from the top. A one and a two and a—no tears—justa sing.*"

That little routine kept us laughing, all the way to the choir loft.

The day of the funeral, we printed out the music to be handed out as people entered. Then we gave a copy to the organist. Cousin Tommy, ever the businessman came up to the choir loft with us. When the organist protested that this was not traditional funeral Mass music, he placed a crisp bill on the organ and said, "For your troubles." Then he left to resume his role as a pallbearer.

Music started. People stood in their pews. We stood at the edge of the balcony. Below the priest opened with, "Please let's all rise as we sing, 'Now thank we God, the strife is o're.'"

That was my cue to lean over the balcony railing and practically shout, "Father, there has been a change. Our first song is "How Great Thou Art." The organist played. Voices filled the church singing "On Eagle's Wings" and "Let there be peace on earth." And Grandma joined Grandpa in grand musical style.

Music, memories, and the Love List

When it was time to say good bye to Poppy, our own father, we gathered around and played his favorite Frank Sinatra tunes. His funeral service was characterized by family and friends telling stories about the man they loved. And we ended by singing a song that captured his personality:

Why are there so many songs about rainbows and what's on the other side."
Rainbows are visions. And only illusions. Rainbows have nothing to hide."
So I've been told and I choose to believe it. But I know it's wrong wait and see.
Someday we'll find it. The rainbow connection, the lovers, the dreamers and me."

Our mother's funeral was a Catholic Mass at Our Lady of the Assumption in Brookline, Massachusetts. Unlike her own mother, she tried to maintain control to the very end. This is an excerpt from my *Psychology Today.com* column.

"THE LOVE LIST AND THE LAST LIST"

Our mother was a list maker. Her lists were often on the back of envelopes. Even when the memory thief slipped into her life, she remembered to make her lists. She was so consumed by her need to buy food and cook, that even as she lay in a semi-comatose state, when my niece Carrie from California flew in to see her she said, "What shall I make you for supper?" To our Mother, food was her love gift.

What is on your love list?

The love list concept is perhaps not new. What is new, however, is how we each choose to devise a list for ourselves that enhances our own lives and the lives of those we love. In our heart of hearts, we all know what we should be doing to bring harmony into our own life and the lives of those around us. Ancient philosophers have long told us:

* Speak kindly to everyone you meet. We all carry a heavy burden.
* Wish blessings to others, even those who hurt you.

* Be forgiving of everyone who has ever hurt you.
* Forgive yourself without second guessing and asking: "Why didn't I?"
* Express your love to those whom you love, instead of saying, "They know I love them"
* Form the words, " I love you."
* Remind yourself often throughout the day that those you love are a gift and you have no idea just how long they will be yours to cherish.

In our mother's case—as with our father—all of the children and grandchildren made a trip to visit when we thought the end was approaching. All of us will cling to words that will bring a smile to our faces.

This thought reminded me of words from our mother's mother, "Never let the sun set on your anger."

If we live the love list, it will be our most important list. Our last list will most likely be a list of unfinished business and it will remain so. However, expressing love—in words and actions—will live in our hearts forever.

Our parents wedding day, September 12, 1942

Our mother's class photo.
She is third from the left in the front row.

From our mother, The Italian Family Christmas was created

We have many wonderful Nanny and Poppy memories and try to recreate growing up moments whenever possible. What follows is a way for you to create treasured memories of your own.

Grandchildren took a silly photo
because Nanny and Poppy loved Christmas fun.

This is a page from the photo album that our sister Lois created.
Find any one family photo of you own and you will find a way to
start your mini-memoir.

Mini-Memoir Writing Guide: Step-by-Step

Whenever anyone asks: "How do you write a memoir?" my answer is always the same—one story at a time. Whenever you say, "I wish I could write about the wonderful memories that I have of growing up," tell a family member or a friend. Let it become a part of your oral tradition. Then once it is spoken, it is easier to sit down and write it just as you would like to treasure the memory for yourself and others.

Most often people say, "I don't know where to start." If you are hoping to recreate Sunday dinner at grandma's. Expand upon that memory.

- Describe the dining room and the table.
- Talk about who came to Sunday dinner.
- Were there special plates used for week-ends only?
- Who usually attended Sunday dinner?
- What did Grandma serve?
- Were you happy to be there?

Here is a brief memory of my grandmother's table:
Our grandparents believed in Sunday dinner together. Gram's homemade pasta was a daily staple. But on holidays, at Thanksgiving, the turkey shared a place with her ravioli. The Christmas goose always sat facing her manicotti. The Easter leg of lamb was nestled next to her lasagna.

In her dining room, Gram said, we could learn about people and love.

Sitting around the welcome table she helped us perfect the art of reading expressions on people's faces—listening to the questions they asked or did not ask, and understanding their laughter, snickers, and silence. She would remind us to watch for sadness or tension in case she missed seeing something when she was back in the pantry getting more food to bring to the table.

Grandma believed that the table was sacred. No matter how much we may have disagreed with one another during the day, she was convinced that any argument could be settled at her table. Even before dinner, when she sensed tension, she magically produced a cup of hot demitasse and freshly made biscotti.

"Mangia. Mangia. Try this for me," she would say. And who could refuse her?

With a kitchen filled with baking breads and pastry treasures, we knew that once she said, "Sit. Eat," whatever ill feelings may have been brewing within us would simply dissipate.

EDITING A MEMORY:

However, some feelings are not pleasant ones. Here is how gratitude can help you edit an unhappy memory simply by rewriting it.

What if you loved going to Grandma's but there was one Aunt who always called you, "her little fatty" and it made you angry? In your mind, or on paper, stand up to the Aunt and instead of feeling shamed or bitter, see yourself as beautiful with plump rosy cheeks. Say to her, "I really like the way I look. So please stop calling me, 'a little fatty.'"

Where you write a mini-memoir, you can include this—because in the world of creative non-fiction, you can tell the story of the hurtful Aunt and then add, "I still remember wanting to stand up to her. And maybe I will right now—if not in person, then in this mini-memoir."

Then begin focusing on all of the goodness that was around the dining room table, the friendship, the laughter, and the food and express gratitude. Grateful people are found to be generally happier, with more social connections and fewer bouts of depression according to the National Institute of Mental Health.

But what happens if you just cannot find your smile? This is when Robert A. Emmons, Ph.D., a professor of psychology at University of California at Davis, would remind us: "Gratitude is an attitude, not a feeling that can be easily willed. By living the gratitude that we do not necessarily feel, we can begin to feel that gratitude that we live."

YOUR MINI-MEMOIR

In a "Memories to Treasure" class that I taught for octogenarians at an assisted living center in 2014, I selected a picture and residents would write whatever came to mind. Although their short-term memories had begun to fail them, photos helped them vividly recall events of their past. We used photos according to a special event of each month—from Valentines to pumpkins, from school days to the Fourth of July.

A favorite photo was the classic sailor kissing a nurse on VJ Day on August 14, 1945. Taken by Alfred Eisenstaedt, it is a photo that evokes memories of "where were you on this day." We would talk about the photo for about 15 minutes as they recalled events. One woman claimed that she was the nurse in the photo. Another insisted, "You were not. I was there." After the kerfuffe, each person created a handwritten, one-page memory in half an hour. Later we word-processed their writing, added a unique picture to each story and framed the works.

When interviewing elderly relatives, it is important to accept what they remember. Even if their memory may not be quite accurate, it is their memory to treasure.

Here is a simple 7 step method that you can use to record special events, holidays, or even a quiet moment when you walked along the beach, or stopped to listen to a bird, or attended an event for a child or grandchild.

Read through the seven steps. And instead of writing first tell your story to someone. It will also give you the confidence to "own" the story before writing about it.

1. Start by thinking about the photograph, a remembered image, or a place that conjures up a special memory.
2. Write about the feelings that enveloped you. Does a smile come to your face? Do you tingle with excitement?
3. Describe the place of the special memory. Was it in your home? Was it in the city or out in the country? Add important sensory details. The smells of the country air, the waves washing against a rock, sounds of honking horns, birds chirping.
4. Who are the important people in your image or photograph? What did they look like? How were they dressed? Describe the expressions on their faces.

5. Listen for their words, the way they spoke. Recreate a few lines of the dialogue that convey their ideas—or expressions that are particular to their region.
6. Explain why you are grateful for the memory.
7. How can you expand the memory?

AFTER THE 7 STEPS—DEVELOP EVEN FURTHER

1. Talk to family members, see what they remember of the moment or event about which you are writing.
2. In one of my stories I learned that a philandering uncle was never labeled a cad, it was simply said that had a "tendency."
3. Try to discover family secrets, patterns, traditions, or beliefs.
4. After talking with others, write your memory in just a page or two.
5. Show your story to other family members whom you trust and see if they agree or disagree. Edit as necessary but trust your own instincts. Remember, you may never again feel a need to share your writing with them. And you do not need to follow their advice.
6. What if others disagree with your point of view? Listen respectfully. However, keep in mind that no two people remember a story in the same way. Hold onto your own version. It's a memory that belongs to you and no one else.
7. After talking with family, did you learn more than you expected? If so, start another story. For example, my uncle's tendency piqued my curiosity and I wanted to learn more about him. It turned out, he was quite a ladies' man.
8. When you are pleased with what you have written, and you think you would like to create a collection, develop an outline.
9. Decide on a time frame; for example, a year in your life as a child, or just summertime memories as a teenager.
10. Do you want the memoir to take place in your family home or neighborhood? If so, describe every important detail that comes to mind. Do some research about things you

have forgotten: street names, neighbor's names, distinct features such as gardens, stores, libraries, even trees that lined the streets.

11. Search for family recipes or old attic treasures.
12. Begin collecting old family photos or photos from the era or neighborhood that you would like to write about.
13. Put the stories together linking them chronologically or thematically. For example, if one story is about playing "Hide and Seek," the next might be about "Learning to Ride a Bike."
14. Give your memoir collection a title and put the stories together.
15. Go to a copy center and have the stories wire bound even if the collection is just for you to keep. What will happen is that you will come to see how a little book emerges. It will encourage you to continue a family history search.

If you are recording stories for a parent or relative and you know what they are saying is not entirely true, what should you do? Smile and express gratitude that they are sharing the memory with you. Respect their imagination and what it is that they wish to convey and believe. We all remember things differently. It is important that you listen, smile, and do not contradict.

In thinking about your own story, if you have a painful memory, write it and then change the ending to something positive. It that cheating? No, it is simply a form of image rescripting which researchers have noted is useful for those who suffer from nightmares or traumatic memories.

However, it can be easier to begin by writing memories for which you are grateful, memories you wish to treasure. As you think about them, talk about them, and write about them, the magic of memories will unfold.

Our parents on their anniversary.

ACKNOWLEDGMENTS

Many of the photos here are from an album that Lois Ardito, her sister, compiled for their parents when the memory thief slipped into their lives. The book itself was edited within the calm beauty and blessings of Youville House in Cambridge, Massachusetts.

This memoir is of the creative non-fiction genre because we all remember events a bit differently. It is with deep appreciation to Ed Iannuccilli, author of *Growing Up Italian: Grandfather's Fig Tree and Other Stories*. He has been a support, an inspiration, and a blessing.

Gratitude to former Suffolk University colleagues:

- Olivia Kate-Cerrone, author of *The Hunger Saint* (Bordighera Press).
- Ben Tanaka, now teaching at the University of Houston.
- George Kalogeris, PhD, and Gail Hanlon, MFA.

Millioni di ringraziamenti to Professor Anthony Tamburri of the Calandra Institute for believing in this book and Nicholas Grosso of Bordighera Press for his direction and patience.

This book reads best with a cappuccino and biscotti.

Rita Watson at Boston's North End. Photo by Lois Ardito.

ABOUT THE AUTHOR

Rita Esposito Watson, the author of six books, has been writing "With Love and Gratitude" for *Psychology Today.com* since 2011. She was also a columnist for *The Providence Journal* for more than 10 years. There Robert Whitcomb, vice president of the *Journal* encouraged her to write her family stories as did Alan Rosenberg, executive editor.

She received a Journalism in Aging Fellows Award in 2012 and a travel grant in 2013 from New American Media with the Gerontological Society of American Media.

After moving to Boston, she served as Director of Communications for CIMIT, an academic and medical partnership with industry and government through Partners.

She has an M.P.H. from the Department of Epidemiology and Public Health, Yale School of Medicine. A long-time family policy advocate, she has been a guest on numerous talk shows, including NBC's The Today Show.

VIA FOLIOS

A refereed book series dedicated to the culture of Italians and Italian Americans.

SARA FRUNER. *Bitter Bites from Sugar Hills*. Vol. 135. Poetry. $12
KATHY CURTO. *Not for Nothing*. Vol. 134. Memoir. $16
JENNIFER MARTELLI. *My Tarantella*. Vol. 133. Poetry. $10
MARIA TERRONE. *At Home in the New World*. Vol. 132. Essays. $16
GIL FAGIANI. *Missing Madonnas*. Vol. 131. Poetry. $12
LEWIS TURCO. *The Sonnetarium*. Vol. 130. Poetry. $12
JOE AMATO. *Samuel Taylor's Hollywood Adventure*. Vol. 129. Novel. $20
BEA TUSIANI. *Con Amore*. Vol. 128. Memoir. $16
MARIA GIURA. *What My Father Taught Me*. Vol. 127. Poetry. $12
STANISLAO PUGLIESE. *A Century of Sinatra*. Vol. 126. Criticism. $12
TONY ARDIZZONE. *The Arab's Ox*. Vol. 125. Novel. $18
PHYLLIS CAPELLO. *Packs Small Plays Big*. Vol. 124. Literature. $10
FRED GARDAPHÉ. *Read 'em and Reap*. Vol. 123. Criticism. $22
JOSEPH A. AMATO. *Diagnostics*. Vol 122. Literature. $12
DENNIS BARONE. *Second Thoughts*. Vol 121. Poetry. $10
OLIVIA K. CERRONE. *The Hunger Saint*. Vol 120. Novella. $12
GARIBLADI M. LAPOLLA. *Miss Rollins in Love*. Vol 119. Novel. $24
JOSEPH TUSIANI. *A Clarion Call*. Vol 118. Poetry. $16
JOSEPH A. AMATO. *My Three Sicilies*. Vol 117. Poetry & Prose. $17
MARGHERITA COSTA. *Voice of a Virtuosa and Coutesan*. Vol 116. Poetry. $24
NICOLE SANTALUCIA. *Because I Did Not Die*. Vol 115. Poetry. $12
MARK CIABATTARI. *Preludes to History*. Vol 114. Poetry. $12
HELEN BAROLINI. *Visits*. Vol 113. Novel. $22
ERNESTO LIVORNI. *The Fathers' America*. Vol 112. Poetry. $14
MARIO B. MIGNONE. *The Story of My People*. Vol 111. Non-fiction. $17
GEORGE GUIDA. *The Sleeping Gulf*. Vol 110. Poetry. $14
JOEY NICOLETTI. *Reverse Graffiti*. Vol 109. Poetry. $14
GIOSE RIMANELLI. *Il mestiere del furbo*. Vol 108. Criticism. $20
LEWIS TURCO. *The Hero Enkidu*. Vol 107. Poetry. $14
AL TACCONELLI. *Perhaps Fly*. Vol 106. Poetry. $14
RACHEL GUIDO DEVRIES. *A Woman Unknown in Her Bones*. Vol 105. Poetry. $11
BERNARD BRUNO. *A Tear and a Tear in My Heart*. Vol 104. Non-fiction. $20
FELIX STEFANILE. *Songs of the Sparrow*. Vol 103. Poetry. $30
FRANK POLIZZI. *A New Life with Bianca*. Vol 102. Poetry. $10
GIL FAGIANI. *Stone Walls*. Vol 101. Poetry. $14
LOUISE DESALVO. *Casting Off*. Vol 100. Fiction. $22
MARY JO BONA. *I Stop Waiting for You*. Vol 99. Poetry. $12
RACHEL GUIDO DEVRIES. *Stati zitt, Josie*. Vol 98. Children's Literature. $8
GRACE CAVALIERI. *The Mandate of Heaven*. Vol 97. Poetry. $14
MARISA FRASCA. *Via incanto*. Vol 96. Poetry. $12

DOUGLAS GLADSTONE. *Carving a Niche for Himself*. Vol 95. History. $12

MARIA TERRONE. *Eye to Eye*. Vol 94. Poetry. $14

CONSTANCE SANCETTA. *Here in Cerchio*. Vol 93. Local History. $15

MARIA MAZZIOTTI GILLAN. *Ancestors' Song*. Vol 92. Poetry. $14

MICHAEL PARENTI. *Waiting for Yesterday: Pages from a Street Kid's Life*. Vol 90. Memoir. $15

ANNIE LANZILLOTTO. *Schistsong*. Vol 89. Poetry. $15

EMANUEL DI PASQUALE. *Love Lines*. Vol 88. Poetry. $10

CAROSONE & LOGIUDICE. *Our Naked Lives*. Vol 87. Essays. $15

JAMES PERICONI. *Strangers in a Strange Land: A Survey of Italian-Language American Books*.Vol 86. Book History. $24

DANIELA GIOSEFFI. *Escaping La Vita Della Cucina*. Vol 85. Essays. $22

MARIA FAMÀ. *Mystics in the Family*. Vol 84. Poetry. $10

ROSSANA DEL ZIO. *From Bread and Tomatoes to Zuppa di Pesce "Ciambotto"*.Vol. 83. $15

LORENZO DELBOCA. *Polentoni*. Vol 82. Italian Studies. $15

SAMUEL GHELLI. *A Reference Grammar*. Vol 81. Italian Language. $36

ROSS TALARICO. *Sled Run*. Vol 80. Fiction. $15

FRED MISURELLA. *Only Sons*. Vol 79. Fiction. $14

FRANK LENTRICCHIA. *The Portable Lentricchia*. Vol 78. Fiction. $16

RICHARD VETERE. *The Other Colors in a Snow Storm*. Vol 77. Poetry. $10

GARIBALDI LAPOLLA. *Fire in the Flesh*. Vol 76 Fiction & Criticism. $25

GEORGE GUIDA. *The Pope Stories*. Vol 75 Prose. $15

ROBERT VISCUSI. *Ellis Island*. Vol 74. Poetry. $28

ELENA GIANINI BELOTTI. *The Bitter Taste of Strangers Bread*. Vol 73. Fiction. $24

PINO APRILE. *Terroni*. Vol 72. Italian Studies. $20

EMANUEL DI PASQUALE. *Harvest*. Vol 71. Poetry. $10

ROBERT ZWEIG. *Return to Naples*. Vol 70. Memoir. $16

AIROS & CAPPELLI. *Guido*. Vol 69. Italian/American Studies. $12

FRED GARDAPHÉ. *Moustache Pete is Dead! Long Live Moustache Pete!*. Vol 67. Literature/Oral History. $12

PAOLO RUFFILLI. *Dark Room/Camera oscura*. Vol 66. Poetry. $11

HELEN BAROLINI. *Crossing the Alps*. Vol 65. Fiction. $14

COSMO FERRARA. *Profiles of Italian Americans*. Vol 64. Italian Americana. $16

GIL FAGIANI. *Chianti in Connecticut*. Vol 63. Poetry. $10

BASSETTI & D'ACQUINO. *Italic Lessons*. Vol 62. Italian/American Studies. $10

CAVALIERI & PASCARELLI, Eds. *The Poet's Cookbook*. Vol 61. Poetry/Recipes. $12

EMANUEL DI PASQUALE. *Siciliana*. Vol 60. Poetry. $8

NATALIA COSTA, Ed. *Bufalini*. Vol 59. Poetry. $18.

RICHARD VETERE. *Baroque*. Vol 58. Fiction. $18.

LEWIS TURCO. *La Famiglia/The Family*. Vol 57. Memoir. $15

NICK JAMES MILETI. *The Unscrupulous*. Vol 56. Humanities. $20

BASSETTI. ACCOLLA. D'AQUINO. *Italici: An Encounter with Piero Bassetti*. Vol 55. Italian Studies. $8

GIOSE RIMANELLI. *The Three-legged One*. Vol 54. Fiction. $15
CHARLES KLOPP. *Bele Antiche Stòrie*. Vol 53. Criticism. $25
JOSEPH RICAPITO. *Second Wave*. Vol 52. Poetry. $12
GARY MORMINO. *Italians in Florida*. Vol 51. History. $15
GIANFRANCO ANGELUCCI. *Federico F*. Vol 50. Fiction. $15
ANTHONY VALERIO. *The Little Sailor*. Vol 49. Memoir. $9
ROSS TALARICO. *The Reptilian Interludes*. Vol 48. Poetry. $15
RACHEL GUIDO DE VRIES. *Teeny Tiny Tino's Fishing Story*. Vol 47.
  Children's Literature. $6
EMANUEL DI PASQUALE. *Writing Anew*. Vol 46. Poetry. $15
MARIA FAMÀ. *Looking For Cover*. Vol 45. Poetry. $12
ANTHONY VALERIO. *Toni Cade Bambara's One Sicilian Night*. Vol 44.
  Poetry. $10
EMANUEL CARNEVALI. *Furnished Rooms*. Vol 43. Poetry. $14
BRENT ADKINS. et al., Ed. *Shifting Borders. Negotiating Places*. Vol 42.
  Conference. $18
GEORGE GUIDA. *Low Italian*. Vol 41. Poetry. $11
GARDAPHÈ, GIORDANO, TAMBURRI. *Introducing Italian Americana*. Vol
  40. Italian/American Studies. $10
DANIELA GIOSEFFI. *Blood Autumn/Autunno di sangue*. Vol 39. Poetry. $15/$25
FRED MISURELLA. *Lies to Live By*. Vol 38. Stories. $15
STEVEN BELLUSCIO. *Constructing a Bibliography*. Vol 37. Italian
  Americana. $15
ANTHONY JULIAN TAMBURRI, Ed. *Italian Cultural Studies 2002*. Vol 36.
  Essays. $18
BEA TUSIANI. *con amore*. Vol 35. Memoir. $19
FLAVIA BRIZIO-SKOV, Ed. *Reconstructing Societies in the Aftermath of War*.
  Vol 34. History. $30
TAMBURRI. et al., Eds. *Italian Cultural Studies 2001*. Vol 33. Essays. $18
ELIZABETH G. MESSINA, Ed. *In Our Own Voices*. Vol 32. Italian/
  American Studies. $25
STANISLAO G. PUGLIESE. *Desperate Inscriptions*. Vol 31. History. $12
HOSTERT & TAMBURRI, Eds. *Screening Ethnicity*. Vol 30. Italian/
  American Culture. $25
G. PARATI & B. LAWTON, Eds. *Italian Cultural Studies*. Vol 29. Essays. $18
HELEN BAROLINI. *More Italian Hours*. Vol 28. Fiction. $16
FRANCO NASI, Ed. *Intorno alla Via Emilia*. Vol 27. Culture. $16
ARTHUR L. CLEMENTS. *The Book of Madness & Love*. Vol 26. Poetry. $10
JOHN CASEY, et al. *Imagining Humanity*. Vol 25. Interdisciplinary Studies. $18
ROBERT LIMA. *Sardinia/Sardegna*. Vol 24. Poetry. $10
DANIELA GIOSEFFI. *Going On*. Vol 23. Poetry. $10
ROSS TALARICO. *The Journey Home*. Vol 22. Poetry. $12
EMANUEL DI PASQUALE. *The Silver Lake Love Poems*. Vol 21. Poetry. $7
JOSEPH TUSIANI. *Ethnicity*. Vol 20. Poetry. $12
JENNIFER LAGIER. *Second Class Citizen*. Vol 19. Poetry. $8
FELIX STEFANILE. *The Country of Absence*. Vol 18. Poetry. $9
PHILIP CANNISTRARO. *Blackshirts*. Vol 17. History. $12

LUIGI RUSTICHELLI, Ed. *Seminario sul racconto*. Vol 16. Narrative. $10

LEWIS TURCO. *Shaking the Family Tree*. Vol 15. Memoirs. $9

LUIGI RUSTICHELLI, Ed. *Seminario sulla drammaturgia*. Vol 14. Theater/ Essays. $10

FRED GARDAPHÈ. *Moustache Pete is Dead! Long Live Moustache Pete!*. Vol 13. Oral Literature. $10

JONE GAILLARD CORSI. *Il libretto d'autore. 1860–1930*. Vol 12. Criticism. $17

HELEN BAROLINI. *Chiaroscuro: Essays of Identity*. Vol 11. Essays. $15

PICARAZZI & FEINSTEIN, Eds. *An African Harlequin in Milan*. Vol 10. Theater/Essays. $15

JOSEPH RICAPITO. *Florentine Streets & Other Poems*. Vol 9. Poetry. $9

FRED MISURELLA. *Short Time*. Vol 8. Novella. $7

NED CONDINI. *Quartettsatz*. Vol 7. Poetry. $7

ANTHONY JULIAN TAMBURRI, Ed. *Fuori: Essays by Italian/American Lesbiansand Gays*. Vol 6. Essays. $10

ANTONIO GRAMSCI. P. Verdicchio. Trans. & Intro. *The Southern Question*. Vol 5.Social Criticism. $5

DANIELA GIOSEFFI. *Word Wounds & Water Flowers*. Vol 4. Poetry. $8

WILEY FEINSTEIN. *Humility's Deceit: Calvino Reading Ariosto Reading Calvino*. Vol 3. Criticism. $10

PAOLO A. GIORDANO, Ed. *Joseph Tusiani: Poet. Translator. Humanist*. Vol 2. Criticism. $25

ROBERT VISCUSI. *Oration Upon the Most Recent Death of Christopher Columbus*. Vol 1. Poetry.

CPSIA information can be obtained
at www.ICGtesting.com
Printed in the USA
FSHW021825120219
55567FS

9 781599 541327